INSOMNIAC

Trials of The Vision

Vee the Vision

Made with ❤ on the BookLeaf Publishing Platform
www.bookleafpub.in
www.bookleafpub.com

Dedication

To Darren

To Anthony

To Ryan

To the rebellious voices that dare to challenge the status quo, who ignite change with their words and actions. To those who speak truth to power, who inspire us to think critically and act boldly. Your courage fuels the fire of progress, reminding us that in defiance lies the potential for transformation. This book is for you—may your echoes resonate through every page and inspire generations to come.

Preface

For some reason, our best and our worst thoughts both come to us at night. The poems in this book are based on those thoughts.

Cover Art by BRIE MAXON

Acknowledgements

I would like to extend my heartfelt gratitude to those who have inspired and supported me throughout this journey. First and foremost, Tupac Shakur and Stan Lee have profoundly shaped my creative spirit. Tupac's powerful words and unyielding passion for justice have taught me the importance of authenticity and resilience. Stan Lee's imaginative storytelling and ability to create worlds filled with heroes have ignited my love for storytelling and the belief that anyone can be a hero in their own right.

I am incredibly grateful to my partner, Brie, whose unwavering support and encouragement have been my anchor. Your belief in my dreams has fueled my ambition, and I cannot thank you enough for standing by my side through every challenge.

To my close friends and brothers—Martin, Leo, Manny, Dare, Jose P., Teddy, Sixx, Camacho, and Tony—thank you for being my creative companions and sounding boards. Your camaraderie, laughter, and shared passion for art and life have enriched my experience immeasurably. Each of you has played a vital role in this journey, and I am blessed to have you in my life.

This book is a testament to the influences and connections that have shaped me, and I dedicate it to all of you. Thank you for being a part of my story.

1. LOOK AT US NOW

You are not alone,
The plot and tone have stopped and grown to make us
the heroes of this story,
The zeroes and the dorks, we
fear no men with forced needs of living among the
mundane,
Sun, rain, adjacent phrases,
space and time couldn't age us
as long as the pages
embrace us the way nobody else did,
"Go to hell, kid!",
They said it but I felt it,
That fire inside of me melted the cell that they tried to
cage us with,
A bully couldn't fully comprehend the comic trend
because for them the topic ends when the status does,
the difference between that and us
is we wear masks to reveal our identities,
Imagination boosts exaggerated truths,
Captivated proof of the human condition,
We were the few men and women who would use them
to visit our true deposition of reality,
Now we're troops with a vision of harmony,
Pardon me if the guard in me is a bit hardened, see

a few years before this started, we

weren't the most regarded, be

that as it may,

Today we have escaped the box they locked us in,

Those who still judge might throw the book at us now,

But you are not alone, LOOK AT US NOW.

2. INKED BLADE

The pen and sword are parallel,
Dare to tell me different?
Whoever said words don't hurt has never carved into
stone for them to stick,
Quick!
Name a moment where the main component didn't
consist of a phrase devoted to tame your motives,
Your brain decoded by the same opponent who knows
their target,
Psychological warfare sheds more blood than when the
Corps floods the desert or jungle,
The pressure can crumble any barriers that stumble upon
it's path,
It's in your pocket, under your thumbs,
Wonder encompasses thunderous supplements funded
with government tactics,
Classic,
Drastic measures seem farfetched but that bar stretches
further,
Archers can murder but artists and wordsmiths can
spark us with courage or tarnish your worth if you let
them,
Pretty words are used to describe hideous tendencies,
Men can see what they pretend to be for their relentless

needs,
So either look both ways before crossing my mind or
wait for the pen to bleed.

3. TIME IS INSTRUMENTAL

I am my own instrument,
My objective is to be blunt because
Streets run through me like they're running out of time,
To doubt a mind is toxicity boxed into a paradox,
Tear approximately into me to make an era stop,
Errors got us programmed with the wrong data,
The wrong place at the right time might chime our own doom,
I'll pluck the strings they tie me with to make my own tune,
The throne room raided and riddled by maidens and fiddlers,
Laid in the middle is the crown for the taking,
The sounds that we're making are the only things to listen to,
JUST LISTEN...

4. BRUJERÍA

Lone man on the run,
Old man with a gun pointed at me sayin'
'What you doin round here?'
'What you doin round here?'

I told him;
It's a little bit complicated
'Cause I'm a little intoxicated
with thoughts of a woman that been flowing through my
blood stream,
Must be a bit a dark magic,
the havoc is passin' it's way through my actions,
Audacities grabbing a hold of my imagination,
Pacin' back and forth with a trace of her fragrance,
It's amazing how she got me fading
In and out of reality, passively dancing around a question
I already know has an answer,
Guess I'm just a man and can only be candid,
This isn't how I planned it,
Then the man said;

'What you doin round here?'
'What you doin round here?'

I told him;
It's a little bit complicated
I just wanna get intoxicated

5. HINDSIGHT

8

Contemplation of complications
consummate the brainstorm of guilt and frustration,
Built with lust, hatred,
and filled with what's wasted
in suppression,
The question is when does the wreckage become
accepted and by whom?

6. ABOVE AND BELOW

9

Above or below.
Where do we stand?
Is the question subjective?
Where do we land
when we fall?
Is the sky the limit if given the chance?
Are we given advances for livin' as passively as we can
manage?
Is patience the true test to prove who's best
In this blue depth of life?
Still waiting for an answer,
Did I pass yet?
The asset's vast, yet it feels so damn set!

7. SONGBIRD

When my rights ears ringing
I hear singing,
The sound of your voice
lets me rejoice,
But I have this fear stinging
On the back of my mind while I'm sitting here thinking,
That it doesn't really matter 'cause I have a clear link
into your heart
and I just wanna hear my songbird,
I just want to listen to my songbird

8. aBRIEviated

Beauty is understated in all the ways that your
Radiance glistens from the persistence of your existence,
Illumination is too adjacent to that of the brightest star
Transcendent to man's question of the sky's limits,
Tenderness for my wishes of your protection,
Affection and effervescence of butterflies in my stomach
are flourishing,
Nourishment of intensions
to call my love pure,
You stand for all above and much more

9. ODE TO STAN

12

When I was fist bumpin' and 16 schemin'
I had Six Hundred and Sixteen reasons
Of morality,
Never really thought that immortality
Existed,
Then I paid attention to consistence,
Convinced that heroes exist, but I've met villains
who forget feelin's when they get dealin',
A malevolent perception set in the
damned dope spot,
It felt irrelevant reading
Stan's Soapbox,
Still empathetic to life choices, the white noise
Is drowned out by my mind's voice,
But I knew the speaker,
A True Believer, who will pass on but still
Tell me more,
A poet, A man, A legend. EXCELSIOR.

10. TAURUS

13

I'm a cancer, she's a Taurus with the purest intentions
Like a muralist,
we can paint this town red, but she ain't no tourist
And I always been curious to endure this
type of relationship
If it came to it,
she's got 17 friends, and I'm all their favorite
But I wouldn't take advantage of the damage that they'd
do
And I know she put me first, but it takes 2
I'd hate to
have to put her in a situation
where she gets to blazin'
'cause she loves me but hates you
That's the basis
She can pack a flame with
how racked her frame is
Bad and dangerous
All dressed up in black and stainless

11. CONCRETE

Dominican pedigree,
heavily in the concrete,
Born and raised in Wash Heights but I know how the
Bronx be,
Whatever it costs me just to prosper the roster,
Keep my posture from the opps 'cause to drop is not
optional,
So before I sell my soul, count to infinity
A bounty for these killing these doubts that they're
giving me,
You can get it twisted with a fountain of Hennessy
and sleep with eyes open like your spouse is your enemy,
I'm no saint but I won't taint,
If I throw flames onto propane,
I'ma use a heat dispenser for these weak agendas,
Infiltrating streets like police arrests in Summer 2020,
Not Even 50 senses could make sums of Many Men see
there isn't plenty friendly when your words cost every
penny,
My first thoughts can be petty
but nobody has to live with them,
This is just the minimum until the tape ends

12. IT'S ALIVE

When I see fire, I turn green,
And I burn schemers with a firm heater,
I'm a nice guy, but a stern leader,
Pack a racket like SERENA,
That's word, FEMA!
At last, the paradox starts,
We crave love but lock hearts
in a box carved
from hot parts,
If war isn't murder will the borders convert us?
The foreigners, the merchants,
The porches, the burners,
The coroners, the churches,
They warn us to burn us,
The torture, the furnace,
Is there more that you heard of?

13. OFTEN

I often wonder if I deserve love
When the softest blunder makes me curve love,
How often have you heard love used in a poem?
A blurred hub of cliches for keepsakes?
My feet stay buried in cemented emotions,
Preventing a notion of deception and knowing
inception has opened a portal to no end,
Paradoxical behavior,
I savor these thoughts as they marinate in my mind,
Care and hate intertwine,
I stare at fate from behind and question its intentions;
Dare I wait or demise?

...

REWIND

...

As I feast eyes on your sweet, kind vessel of embrace,
I face the decline of deceit,
Time is a niche that I'd blindly compete
with if it finally completes
Our lives with a deep dive into your essence.
A lesson I've learned since your entrance
into this question I call life,
The answer you've provided ignited the spark in my
spirit,

If you hear it, it's real,
A mirror can fill our reflections with opposite images,
But difference is common with attraction,
If actions speak volumes, I'll blow out the speakers

14. UNBREAKABLE

Going into Hammer Shock
in Ragnarok,
They clash and drop,
So there's no point to grab the Glock,
Your plan to stop
The wrath of Odinson's
a bogus one,
I'm feeling like the Chosen One,
Is that a metaphor
or am I self absorbed?
I felt the core
heating up like Zelda's sword
or Belphegor,
My repertoire is Supernatural,
I rep the poor to set the score and loot the cash flow,
But if I crush herb for a suit of Vibranium,
Lose the titanium,
Shooter by cranium,
A boost of my premium can levitate your whole army,
And drop them quick
like a Apocalypse
in Metropolis

15. THE BIG PICTURE

My water sign points to self destruction as I pour the
tears from the fire in both eyes.
Do I put it out or let the smoke rise?
It'd be a cold price if hope dies,
Rope ties, gold or not
can't be sold for thought,
Temptation could've had me fooled,
Desperation has before
when I slammed the door on morality
and bagged a score,
That and more
but that's before
I went back and forth
towards the big picture

16. DAY & NIGHTMARE

The American Dream is a nightmare
that might stare
quite clearly
at your deepest desires,
Catered egos mistaken for layered people,
we all have levels
but those who revel
on the hearts of rebels just to settle
for mediocrity
are quite possibly more of a knock to me
than monotony itself,
Keep your heads up and feet down,
the rebound for when you speak now
comes from every angle,
Eyes open and fists closed,
For the distros of misconception

17. FUND THE MENTAL (PARANOIA)

It's fundamental to fund the mental,
I run the pen till my veins leak on paper
while I speak on capers,
Keep my feet off glaciers,
Got receipts on traitors,
Keep the PIECE on tailored
for my PEACE, all in favor
for defeat fall later,
'Cause Karma catches everybody after the fact

18. HE SAID / SHE SAID

Having 2 sides to a coin doesn't give it more value,
I know a couple heads would do anything for a TALE,
Meddling for a sale to the right buyer with the wrong
hand,
The burden of its currency can be refunded
inadvertently,
Certainties are a coin toss,
Avoid loss by not investing

19. BURN ME DOWN

23

I told the world 'don't burn me down', but it threw coal
at the fire
So I walk around with my hat low, dressed in all black
attire,
and just wondering,
if I can ever dare to trust again
when fake friends turn enemies and lovers become just a
friend
who must begin
to forget,
through the midst of it
I'm mischievous,
Thinking about the past and missing it,
can't stand to be alone so I tend to call up different
chicks,
and wish that it was all a bad dream that never took
place,
At least I know the difference between a real smile and a
crook's face,
not to be dramatic, but one minute they hate you,
the next they're all fanatics, but half of the time it ain't
true

20. LEADING LADY

When I see you in that backless
black dress,
My past gets
dimmer like a sinner to a Baptist,
Actresses can have their change of scenery,
and a piece of dialogue,
but there's no room for liars, dawg

So say it right,
day and night
I think about the match that makes the flame ignite,
But you're not in the same play when this movie's on,
and I don't care what they say, just don't prove me
wrong

21. SHADES

You can roleplay as hypocrite,
Throw shade or sit in it,
The choice is yours,
Your voice is yours until it isn't,
My lips tell all without a single word spoken,
A token for my thoughts still won't amount to my
survival,
They have infiltrated perception,
Correction is facilitated,
ill debated from all directions,
If you pick one side it's the wrong one,
Choose love to not defuse love
because the News hub
won't let you,
They remind you to forget you,
But even forgotten history repeats itself,
Defeat can tell
if you're approaching glory,
Just tell the story

www.ingramcontent.com/pod-product-compliance
Lightning Source LLC
LaVergne TN
LVHW051245200726
843510LV00011B/1696